Belongs to : _____

Catholic
Coloring Prayer Journal

52 week guided scripture
and reflection coloring journal

-

undated

D: _____ Things I can learn today:

S

D: _____ I am grateful for:

M

D: _____ How I will serve God's people:

T

D: _____ My strongest emotions right now:

W

D: _____ Ways I feel I am coming up short or far from God:

T

D: _____ Ways I am feeling God's presence:

F

_____ Praying over the week and looking forward:

S

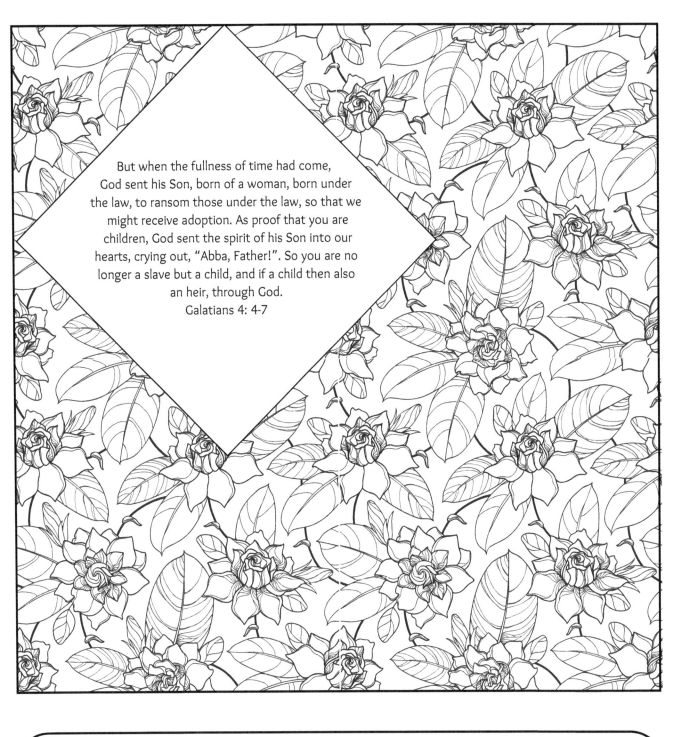

But when the fullness of time had come, God sent his Son, born of a woman, born under the law, to ransom those under the law, so that we might receive adoption. As proof that you are children, God sent the spirit of his Son into our hearts, crying out, "Abba, Father!". So you are no longer a slave but a child, and if a child then also an heir, through God.
Galatians 4: 4-7

Reflection:

D: _____ Scripture I can learn today:

S

D: _____ I am in awe of:

M

D: _____ How I think I am following God's will:

T

D: _____ Frustrations of my day or week to pray over:

W

D: _____ Blessings I request for others:

T

D: _____ Blessings I request for myself:

F

_____ Praying over the week and looking forward:

S

Lord, every nation
on earth will
adore you.
Psalms 72:11

Reflection:

D: _____ Where can I provide help?

S

D: _____ Where can I ask for help?

M

D: _____ What is the greatest challenge God is setting for me right now?

T

D: _____ What is something I can give up for God?

W

D: _____ How can I do a better job of loving others?

T

D: _____ How can I do a better job of loving myself?

F

_____ Praying over the week and looking forward:

S

Paul, called to be an apostle of Jesus Christ by the will of God, and Sosthenes a brother, to the church of God that is at Corinth, to them that are sanctified in Christ Jesus, called to be saints, with all that invoke the name of our Lord Jesus Christ, in every place of theirs and ours. Grace to you, and peace from God our Father, and from the Lord Jesus Christ.

First Corinthians 1:1-3

Reflection:

D: _____ What am I deeply fearing?

S

D: _____ Where am I feeling passion lead me lately?

M

D: _____ In my heart, do I feel that my passion aligns with God's purpose for me?

T

D: _____ How are my fears holding me back from following God's way?

W

D: _____ One step I can take to overcome my fear:

T

D: _____ One specific, actionable goal I can make to follow God's way:

F

_____ Praying over the week and looking forward:

S

One thing I have asked of the Lord, this will I seek after; that I may dwell in the house of the Lord all the days of my life. That I may see the delight of the Lord, and may visit his temple.

Psalms 27: 4

Reflection:

D: _____ I am grateful for:

S

D: _____ How I will serve God's people:

M

D: _____ My strongest emotions right now:

T

D: _____ Ways I feel I am coming up short or far from God:

W

D: _____ Ways I am feeling God's presence:

T

D: _____ Things I can learn today:

F

_____ Praying over the week and looking forward:

S

Seek the LORD, all you humble of
the land, who have observed his
law; seek justice, seek humility;
perhaps you will be sheltered
on the day of the LORD's anger.
Zephaniah 2:3

Reflection:

D: _____ Blessings I request for myself:

S

D: _____ Scripture I can learn today:

M

D: _____ I am in awe of:

T

D: _____ How I think I am following God's will:

W

D: _____ Frustrations of my day or week to pray over:

T

D: _____ Blessings I request for others:

F

_____ Praying over the week and looking forward:

S

And I was with you in weakness, and in fear, and in much trembling. And my speech and my preaching was not in the persuasive words of human wisdom, but in shewing of the Spirit and power; that your faith might not stand on the wisdom of men, but on the power of God.
First Corinthians 2:3-5

Reflection:

D: _____ How can I do a better job of loving myself?

S

D: _____ Where can I provide help?

M

D: _____ Where can I ask for help?

T

D: _____ What is the greatest challenge God is setting for me right now?

W

D: _____ What is something I can give up for God?

T

D: _____ How can I do a better job of loving others?

F

_____ Praying over the week and looking forward:

S

May my ways be firm
in the observance of
your statutes!
Psalms 119:5

Reflection:

D: _____   One specific, actionable goal I can make to follow God's way:

S

D: _____   What am I deeply fearing?

M

D: _____   Where am I feeling passion lead me lately?

T

D: _____   In my heart, do I feel that my passion aligns with God's purpose for me?

W

D: _____   How are my fears holding me back from following God's way?

T

D: _____   One step I can take to overcome my fear:

F

_____   Praying over the week and looking forward:

S

If anyone wants to go to law with you over your tunic, hand him your cloak as well. Should anyone press you into service for one mile, go with him for two miles. Give to the one who asks of you, and do not turn your back on one who wants to borrow.

Matthew 5:40-41

Reflection:

D: _____ How I will serve God's people:

S

D: _____ My strongest emotions right now:

M

D: _____ Ways I feel I am coming up short or far from God:

T

D: _____ Ways I am feeling God's presence:

W

D: _____ Things I can learn today:

T

D: _____ I am grateful for:

F

_____ Praying over the week and looking forward:

S

For if, by the transgression of one person, death came to reign through that one, how much more will those who receive the abundance of grace and of the gift of justification come to reign in life through the one person Jesus Christ.

Romans 5:17

Reflection:

D: _____ Blessings I request for others:

S

D: _____ Blessings I request for myself:

M

D: _____ Scripture I can learn today:

T

D: _____ I am in awe of:

W

D: _____ How I think I am following God's will:

T

D: _____ Frustrations of my day or week to pray over:

F

_____ Praying over the week and looking forward:

S

Our soul waits for the LORD,
he is our help and shield. May
your mercy, LORD, be upon us;
as we put our hope in you.
Psalms 33:20, 22

Reflection:

D: _____ How can I do a better job of loving others?

S

D: _____ How can I do a better job of loving myself?

M

D: _____ Where can I provide help?

T

D: _____ Where can I ask for help?

W

D: _____ What is the greatest challenge God is setting for me right now?

T

D: _____ What is something I can give up for God?

F

_____ Praying over the week and looking forward:

S

Jesus answered and said to her,
"Everyone who drinks this water will
be thirsty again; but whoever drinks
the water I shall give will never thirst;
the water I shall give will become in
him a spring of water welling up to
eternal life."
John 4:13-14

Reflection:

D: _____   One step I can take to overcome my fear:

S

D: _____   One specific, actionable goal I can make to follow God's way:

M

D: _____   What am I deeply fearing?

T

D: _____   Where am I feeling passion lead me lately?

W

D: _____   In my heart, do I feel that my passion aligns with God's purpose for me?

T

D: _____   How are my fears holding me back from following God's way?

F

_____   Praying over the week and looking forward:

S

Solemnity: The Annunciation of the Lord

The Lord is my
shepherd; there is
nothing I lack.
Psalms 23:1

Reflection:

D: _____ Where has God led me over the last twelve weeks?

S

D: _____ How has my faith grown in the last twelve weeks?

M

D: _____ What patterns do I see in my reflections and prayers of last twelve weeks?

T

D: _____ Where do I sense God's presence pulling me for the next twelve weeks?

W

D: _____ How do I want to deepen my faith in the next twelve weeks?

T

D: _____ What are my goals and dreams for the next twelve weeks?

F

_____ Praying over the week and looking forward:

S

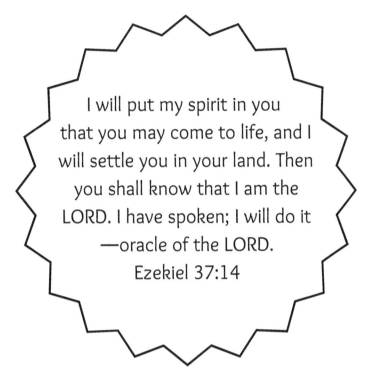

I will put my spirit in you
that you may come to life, and I
will settle you in your land. Then
you shall know that I am the
LORD. I have spoken; I will do it
—oracle of the LORD.
Ezekiel 37:14

Reflection:

D: _____ My strongest emotions right now:

S

D: _____ Ways I feel I am coming up short or far from God:

M

D: _____ Ways I am feeling God's presence:

T

D: _____ Things I can learn today:

W

D: _____ I am grateful for:

T

D: _____ How I will serve God's people:

F

_____ Praying over the week and looking forward:

S

Holy Saturday

The very large crowd spread their cloaks on the road, while others cut branches from the trees and strewed them on the road. The crowds preceding him and those following kept crying out and saying: "Hosanna to the Son of David; blessed is he who comes in the name of the Lord; hosanna in the highest."

Matthew 21:8-9

Reflection:

D: _____ Frustrations of my day or week to pray over:

S

D: _____ Blessings I request for others:

M

D: _____ Blessings I request for myself:

T

D: _____ Scripture I can learn today:

W

D: _____ I am in awe of:

T

D: _____ How I think I am following God's will:

F

_____ Praying over the week and looking forward:

S

To him all the prophets bear witness, that everyone who believes in him will receive forgiveness of sins through his name.
Acts 10:43

Reflection:

D: _____ What is something I can give up for God?

S

D: _____ How can I do a better job of loving others?

M

D: _____ How can I do a better job of loving myself?

T

D: _____ Where can I provide help?

W

D: _____ Where can I ask for help?

T

D: _____ What is the greatest challenge God is setting for me right now?

F

_____ Praying over the week and looking forward:

S

When he had said this, he
showed them his hands and
his side. The disciples
rejoiced when they saw the
Lord. Jesus said to them
again, "Peace be with you.
As the Father has sent me,
so I send you."
John 20:20-21

Reflection:

D: _____ How are my fears holding me back from following God's way?

S

D: _____ One step I can take to overcome my fear:

M

D: _____ One specific, actionable goal I can make to follow God's way:

T

D: _____ What am I deeply fearing?

W

D: _____ Where am I feeling passion lead me lately?

T

D: _____ In my heart, do I feel that my passion aligns with God's purpose for me?

F

_____ Praying over the week and looking forward:

S

And it happened that, while he was with them at table, he took bread, said the blessing, broke it, and gave it to them. With that their eyes were opened and they recognized him, but he vanished from their sight. Then they said to each other, "Were not our hearts burning within us while he spoke to us on the way and opened the scriptures to us?" So they set out at once and returned to Jerusalem where they found gathered together the eleven and those with them who were saying, "The Lord has truly been raised and has appeared to Simon!"
Luke 24:30-34

Reflection:

D: _____ Ways I feel I am coming up short or far from God:

S

D: _____ Ways I am feeling God's presence:

M

D: _____ Things I can learn today:

T

D: _____ I am grateful for:

W

D: _____ How I will serve God's people:

T

D: _____ My strongest emotions right now:

F

_____ Praying over the week and looking forward:

S

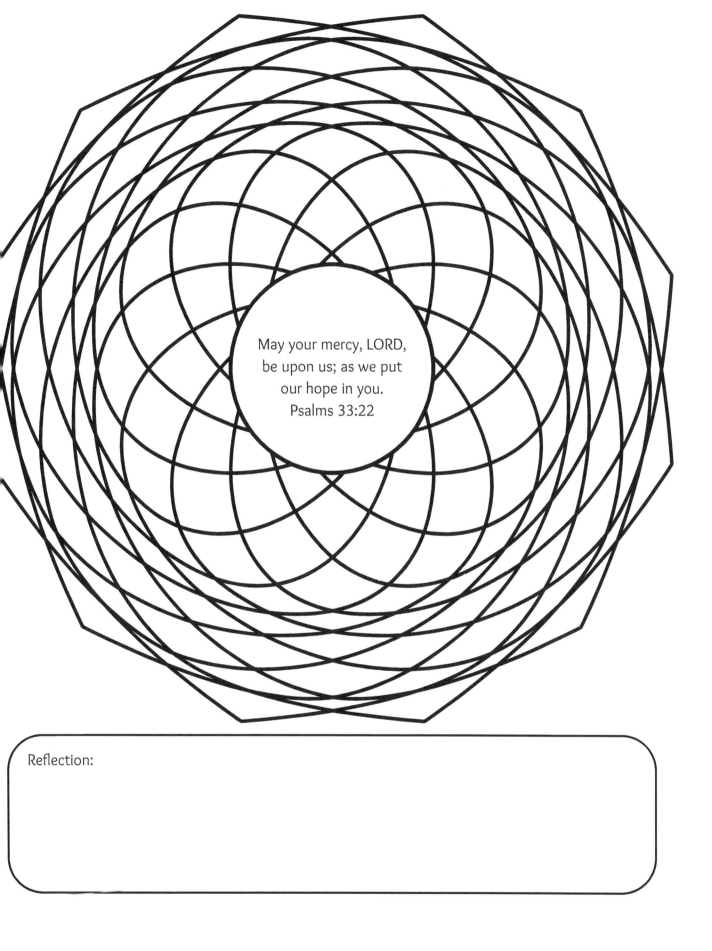

May your mercy, LORD,
be upon us; as we put
our hope in you.
Psalms 33:22

Reflection:

D: _____ How I think I am following God's will:

S

D: _____ Frustrations of my day or week to pray over:

M

D: _____ Blessings I request for others:

T

D: _____ Blessings I request for myself:

W

D: _____ Scripture I can learn today:

T

D: _____ I am in awe of:

F

_____ Praying over the week and looking forward:

S

Whoever has my commandments and observes them is the one who loves me. And whoever loves me will be loved by my Father, and I will love him and reveal myself to him.

John 14:21

Reflection:

D: _____ What is the greatest challenge God is setting for me right now?

S

D: _____ What is something I can give up for God?

M

D: _____ How can I do a better job of loving others?

T

D: _____ How can I do a better job of loving myself?

W

D: _____ Where can I provide help?

T

D: _____ Where can I ask for help?

F

_____ Praying over the week and looking forward:

S

And behold,
I am with you always, until
the end of the age.
Matthew 28:20

Reflection:

D: _____ In my heart, do I feel that my passion aligns with God's purpose for me?

S

D: _____ How are my fears holding me back from following God's way?

M

D: _____ One step I can take to overcome my fear:

T

D: _____ One specific, actionable goal I can make to follow God's way:

W

D: _____ What am I deeply fearing?

T

D: _____ Where am I feeling passion lead me lately?

F

_____ Praying over the week and looking forward:

S

And no one can say, "Jesus is Lord," except by the holy Spirit. There are different kinds of spiritual gifts but the same Spirit; there are different forms of service but the same Lord; there are different workings but the same God who produces all of them in everyone.
1 Corinthians 12:3b-6

Reflection:

D: _____   Ways I am feeling God's presence:

S

D: _____   Things I can learn today:

M

D: _____   I am grateful for:

T

D: _____   How I will serve God's people:

W

D: _____   My strongest emotions right now:

T

D: _____   Ways I feel I am coming up short or far from God:

F

_____   Praying over the week and looking forward:

S

Blessed are you in the
firmament of heaven,
praiseworthy and glorious
forever.
Daniel 3:56

Reflection:

D: _____ How I think I am following God's will:

S

D: _____ Frustrations of my day or week to pray over:

M

D: _____ Blessings I request for others:

T

D: _____ Blessings I request for myself:

W

D: _____ Scripture I can learn today:

T

D: _____ I am in awe of:

F

_____ Praying over the week and looking forward:

S

The cup of blessing that we bless, is it not a participation in the blood of Christ? The bread that we break, is it not a participation in the body of Christ? Because the loaf of bread is one, we, though many, are one body, for we all partake of the one loaf.

1 Corinthians 10:16-17

Reflection:

D: _____ Where can I ask for help?

S

D: _____ What is the greatest challenge God is setting for me right now?

M

D: _____ What is something I can give up for God?

T

D: _____ How can I do a better job of loving others?

W

D: _____ How can I do a better job of loving myself?

T

D: _____ Where can I provide help?

F

_____ Praying over the week and looking forward:

S

Then he said to his disciples, "The harvest is abundant but the laborers are few; so ask the master of the harvest to send out laborers for his harvest."
Matthew 9:37-38

Reflection:

D: _____ Where am I feeling passion lead me lately?

S

D: _____ In my heart, do I feel that my passion aligns with God's purpose for me?

M

D: _____ How are my fears holding me back from following God's way?

T

D: _____ One step I can take to overcome my fear:

W

D: _____ One specific, actionable goal I can make to follow God's way:

T

D: _____ What am I deeply fearing?

F

_____ Praying over the week and looking forward:

S

Sing to the LORD,
praise the LORD, for he
has rescued the life of the
poor from the power of
the evildoers!
Jeremiah 20:13

Reflection:

D: _____ Where has God led me over the last twelve weeks?

S

D: _____ How has my faith grown in the last twelve weeks?

M

D: _____ What patterns do I see in my reflections and prayers of last twelve weeks?

T

D: _____ Where do I sense God's presence pulling me for the next twelve weeks?

W

D: _____ How do I want to deepen my faith in the next twelve weeks?

T

D: _____ What are my goals and dreams for the next twelve weeks?

F

_____ Praying over the week and looking forward:

S

Therefore do not be afraid of them. Nothing is concealed that will not be revealed, nor secret that will not be known. What I say to you in the darkness, speak in the light; what you hear whispered, proclaim on the housetops.

Matthew 10:26-27

Reflection:

D: _____ Things I can learn today:

S

D: _____ I am grateful for:

M

D: _____ How I will serve God's people:

T

D: _____ My strongest emotions right now:

W

D: _____ Ways I feel I am coming up short or far from God:

T

D: _____ Ways I am feeling God's presence:

F

_____ Praying over the week and looking forward:

S

I will sing of your mercy forever, LORD proclaim your faithfulness through all ages. For I said, "My mercy is established forever; my faithfulness will stand as long as the heavens.
Psalms 89:2-3

Reflection:

D: _____ Scripture I can learn today:

S

D: _____ I am in awe of:

M

D: _____ How I think I am following God's will:

T

D: _____ Frustrations of my day or week to pray over:

W

D: _____ Blessings I request for others:

T

D: _____ Blessings I request for myself:

F

_____ Praying over the week and looking forward:

S

Exult greatly, O daughter Zion! Shout for joy, O daughter Jerusalem! Behold: your king is coming to you, a just savior is he, humble, and riding on a donkey, on a colt, the foal of a donkey. He shall banish the chariot from Ephraim, and the horse from Jerusalem; the warrior's bow will be banished, and he will proclaim peace to the nations. His dominion will be from sea to sea, and from the River to the ends of the earth.

Zechariah 9:9-10

Reflection:

D: _____ Where can I provide help?

S

D: _____ Where can I ask for help?

M

D: _____ What is the greatest challenge God is setting for me right now?

T

D: _____ What is something I can give up for God?

W

D: _____ How can I do a better job of loving others?

T

D: _____ How can I do a better job of loving myself?

F

_____ Praying over the week and looking forward:

S

I consider that the sufferings of this present time are as nothing compared with the glory to be revealed for us. For creation awaits with eager expectation the revelation of the children of God; for creation was made subject to futility, not of its own accord but because of the one who subjected it,o in hope that creation itself would be set free from slavery to corruption and share in the glorious freedom of the children of God.

Romans 8:18-21

Reflection:

D: _____ What am I deeply fearing?

S

D: _____ Where am I feeling passion lead me lately?

M

D: _____ In my heart, do I feel that my passion aligns with God's purpose for me?

T

D: _____ How are my fears holding me back from following God's way?

W

D: _____ One step I can take to overcome my fear:

T

D: _____ One specific, actionable goal I can make to follow God's way:

F

_____ Praying over the week and looking forward:

S

Lord, you are good and forgiving, most merciful to all who call on you.
Psalms 86:5

Reflection:

D: _____ I am grateful for:

S

D: _____ How I will serve God's people:

M

D: _____ My strongest emotions right now:

T

D: _____ Ways I feel I am coming up short or far from God:

W

D: _____ Ways I am feeling God's presence:

T

D: _____ Things I can learn today:

F

_____ Praying over the week and looking forward:

S

We know that all things work
for good for those who love
God, who are called according
to his purpose.
Romans 8:28

Reflection:

D: _____ Blessings I request for myself:

S

D: _____ Scripture I can learn today:

M

D: _____ I am in awe of:

T

D: _____ How I think I am following God's will:

W

D: _____ Frustrations of my day or week to pray over:

T

D: _____ Blessings I request for others:

F

_____ Praying over the week and looking forward:

S

For he received honor and glory from God the Father when that unique declaration came to him from the majestic glory, "This is my Son, my beloved, with whom I am well pleased." We ourselves heard this voice come from heaven while we were with him on the holy mountain. Moreover, we possess the prophetic message that is altogether reliable. You will do well to be attentive to it, as to a lamp shining in a dark place, until day dawns and the morning star rises in your hearts.

2 Peter 1:17-19

Reflection:

D: _____ How can I do a better job of loving myself?

S

D: _____ Where can I provide help?

M

D: _____ Where can I ask for help?

T

D: _____ What is the greatest challenge God is setting for me right now?

W

D: _____ What is something I can give up for God?

T

D: _____ How can I do a better job of loving others?

F

_____ Praying over the week and looking forward:

S

Immediately Jesus stretched out his hand and caught him, and said to him, "O you of little faith, why did you doubt?"
Matthew 14:31

Reflection:

D: _____   One specific, actionable goal I can make to follow God's way?

S

D: _____   What am I deeply fearing?

M

D: _____   Where am I feeling passion lead me lately?

T

D: _____   In my heart, do I feel that my passion aligns with God's purpose for me?

W

D: _____   How are my fears holding me back from following God's way?

T

D: _____   One step I can take to overcome my fear:

F

_____   Praying over the week and looking forward:

S

May the peoples
praise you, God;
may all the peoples
praise you!
Psalms 67:4

Reflection:

D: _____ How I will serve God's people:

S

D: _____ My strongest emotions right now:

M

D: _____ Ways I feel I am coming up short or far from God:

T

D: _____ Ways I am feeling God's presence:

W

D: _____ Things I can learn today:

T

D: _____ I am grateful for:

F

_____ Praying over the week and looking forward:

S

Simon Peter said in reply, "You are the Messiah, the Son of the living God." Jesus said to him in reply, "Blessed are you, Simon son of Jonah. For flesh and blood has not revealed this to you, but my heavenly Father.
Matthew 16:16-17

Reflection:

D: _____   Blessings I request for others:

S

D: _____   Blessings I request for myself:

M

D: _____   Scripture I can learn today:

T

D: _____   I am in awe of:

W

D: _____   How I think I am following God's will:

T

D: _____   Frustrations of my day or week to pray over:

F

_____   Praying over the week and looking forward:

S

I urge you therefore, brothers, by the
mercies of God, to offer your bodies
as a living sacrifice, holy and pleasing
to God, your spiritual worship. Do not
conform yourselves to this age but be
transformed by the renewal of your
mind, that you may discern what is
the will of God, what is good and
pleasing and perfect.
Romans 12:1-2

Reflection:

D: _____ How can I do a better job of loving others?

S

D: _____ How can I do a better job of loving myself?

M

D: _____ Where can I provide help?

T

D: _____ Where can I ask for help?

W

D: _____ What is the greatest challenge God is setting for me right now?

T

D: _____ What is something I can give up for God?

F

_____ Praying over the week and looking forward:

S

Come, let us sing joyfully to the LORD;
cry out to the rock of our salvation. Let us come before
him with a song of praise, joyfully sing out our psalms.
Psalms 95:1-2

Reflection:

D: _____

One step I can take to overcome my fear:

S

D: _____

One specific, actionable goal I can make to follow God's way:

M

D: _____

What am I deeply fearing?

T

D: _____

Where am I feeling passion lead me lately?

W

D: _____

In my heart, do I feel that my passion aligns with God's purpose for me?

T

D: _____

How are my fears holding me back from following God's way?

F

_____

Praying over the week and looking forward:

S

I give you a new commandment: love one another. As I have loved you, so you also should love one another.
John 13:34

Reflection:

D: _____

S

Where has God led me over the last twelve weeks?

D: _____

M

How has my faith grown in the last twelve weeks?

D: _____

T

What patterns do I see in my reflections and prayers of last twelve weeks?

D: _____

W

Where do I sense God's presence pulling me for the next twelve weeks?

D: _____

T

How do I want to deepen my faith in the next twelve weeks?

D: _____

F

What are my goals and dreams for the next twelve weeks?

_____

S

Praying over the week and looking forward:

"'My friend, I am not cheating you. Did you not agree with me for the usual daily wage? Take what is yours and go. What if I wish to give this last one the same as you? Or am I not free to do as I wish with my own money? Are you envious because I am generous?' Thus, the last will be first, and the first will be last."

Matthew 20:13-16

Reflection:

D: _____ My strongest emotions right now:

S

D: _____ Ways I feel I am coming up short or far from God:

M

D: _____ Ways I am feeling God's presence:

T

D: _____ Things I can learn today:

W

D: _____ I am grateful for:

T

D: _____ How I will serve God's people:

F

_____ Praying over the week and looking forward:

S

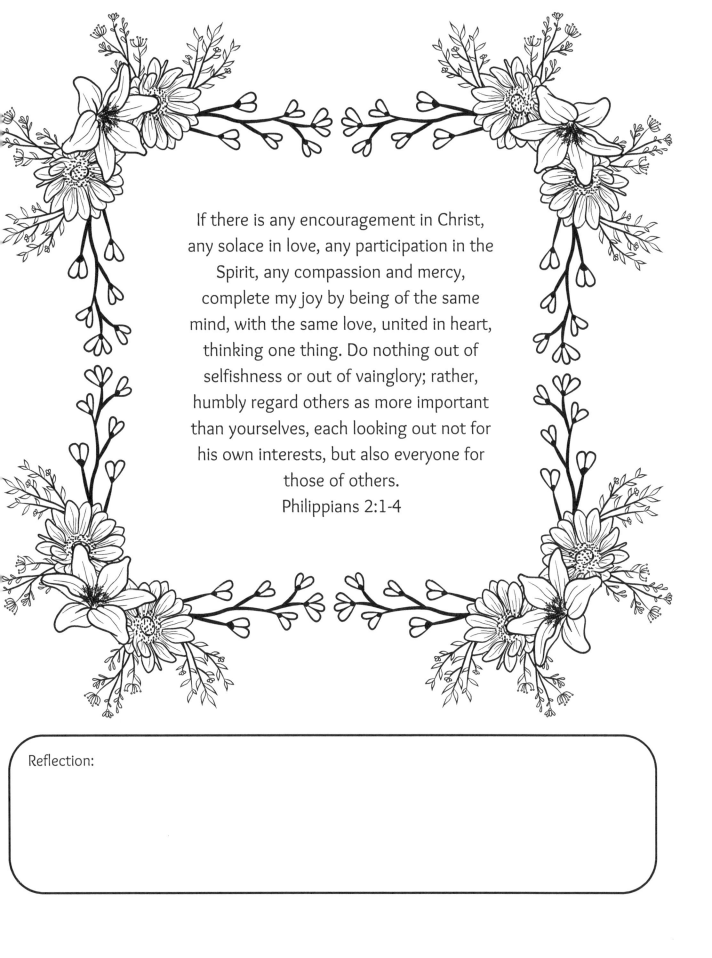

If there is any encouragement in Christ, any solace in love, any participation in the Spirit, any compassion and mercy, complete my joy by being of the same mind, with the same love, united in heart, thinking one thing. Do nothing out of selfishness or out of vainglory; rather, humbly regard others as more important than yourselves, each looking out not for his own interests, but also everyone for those of others.

Philippians 2:1-4

Reflection:

D: _____   Frustrations of my day or week to pray over:

S

D: _____   Blessings I request for others:

M

D: _____   Blessings I request for myself:

T

D: _____   Scripture I can learn today:

W

D: _____   I am in awe of:

T

D: _____   How I think I am following God's will:

F

_____   Praying over the week and looking forward:

S

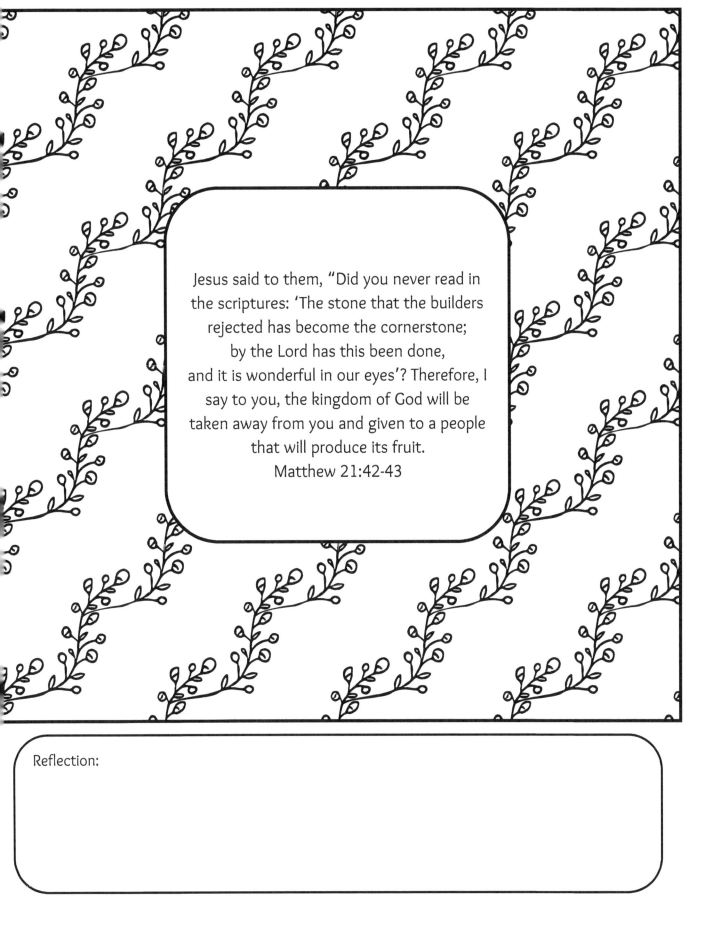

Jesus said to them, "Did you never read in the scriptures: 'The stone that the builders rejected has become the cornerstone; by the Lord has this been done, and it is wonderful in our eyes'? Therefore, I say to you, the kingdom of God will be taken away from you and given to a people that will produce its fruit.
Matthew 21:42-43

Reflection:

D: _____ What is something I can give up for God?

S

D: _____ How can I do a better job of loving others?

M

D: _____ How can I do a better job of loving myself?

T

D: _____ Where can I provide help?

W

D: _____ Where can I ask for help?

T

D: _____ What is the greatest challenge God is setting for me right now?

F

_____ Praying over the week and looking forward:

S

I have the strength for everything through him who empowers me.
Philippians 4:13

Reflection:

D: _____ How are my fears holding me back from following God's way?

S

D: _____ One step I can take to overcome my fear:

M

D: _____ One specific, actionable goal I can make to follow God's way:

T

D: _____ What am I deeply fearing?

W

D: _____ Where am I feeling passion lead me lately?

T

D: _____ In my heart, do I feel that my passion aligns with God's purpose for me?

F

_____ Praying over the week and looking forward:

S

I am the LORD,
there is no other, there is no God
besides me. It is I who arm you,
though you do not know me, so that
all may know, from the rising of the
sun to its setting, that there is none
besides me. I am the LORD, there is
no other.
Isaiah 45:5-6

Reflection:

D: _____ Ways I feel I am coming up short or far from God:

S

D: _____ Ways I am feeling God's presence:

M

D: _____ Things I can learn today:

T

D: _____ I am grateful for:

W

D: _____ How I will serve God's people:

T

D: _____ My strongest emotions right now:

F

_____ Praying over the week and looking forward:

S

He said to him, "You shall love the Lord, your God, with all your heart, with all your soul, and with all your mind. This is the greatest and the first commandment. The second is like it: You shall love your neighbor as yourself. The whole law and the prophets depend on these two commandments."
Matthew 22:37-40

Reflection:

D: _____

S

How I think I am following God's will:

D: _____

M

Frustrations of my day or week to pray over:

D: _____

T

Blessings I request for others:

D: _____

W

Blessings I request for myself:

D: _____

T

Scripture I can learn today:

D: _____

F

I am in awe of:

D: _____

S

Praying over the week and looking forward:

Have we not all one father
Has not one God created
us? Why, then, do we break
faith with each other,
profaning the covenant of
our ancestors?
Malachi 2:10

Reflection:

D: _____

S

What is the greatest challenge God is setting for me right now?

D: _____

M

What is something I can give up for God?

D: _____

T

How can I do a better job of loving others?

D: _____

W

How can I do a better job of loving myself?

D: _____

T

Where can I provide help?

D: _____

F

Where can I ask for help?

_____

Praying over the week and looking forward:

S

O God, you are my God,
it is you I seek! For you my
body yearns; for you my soul
thirsts. In a land parched,
lifeless, and without water.
Psalms 63:2

Reflection:

D: _____

S

In my heart, do I feel that my passion aligns with God's purpose for me?

D: _____

M

How are my fears holding me back from following God's way?

D: _____

T

One step I can take to overcome my fear:

D: _____

W

One specific, actionable goal I can make to follow God's way:

D: _____

T

What am I deeply fearing?

D: _____

F

Where am I feeling passion lead me lately?

_____

S

Praying over the week and looking forward:

But you, brothers, are not in darkness,
for that day to overtake you like a thief.
For all of you are children of the light
and children of the day. We are not of
the night or of darkness. Therefore, let
us not sleep as the rest do, but let us
stay alert and sober.
1 Thessalonians 5:4-6

Reflection:

D: _____

S

Ways I am feeling God's presence:

D: _____

M

Things I can learn today:

D: _____

T

I am grateful for:

D: _____

W

How I will serve God's people:

D: _____

T

My strongest emotions right now:

D: _____

F

Ways I feel I am coming up short or far from God:

_____

S

Praying over the week and looking forward:

For I was hungry and you gave me food, I was thirsty and you gave me drink, a stranger and you welcomed me, naked and you clothed me, ill and you cared for me, in prison and you visited me.' Then the righteous will answer him and say, 'Lord, when did we see you hungry and feed you, or thirsty and give you drink? When did we see you a stranger and welcome you, or naked and clothe you? When did we see you ill or in prison, and visit you?' And the king will say to them in reply, 'Amen, I say to you, whatever you did for one of these least brothers of mine, you did for me.'
Matthew 25:35-40

Reflection:

D: _____ How I think I am following God's will:

S

D: _____ Frustrations of my day or week to pray over:

M

D: _____ Blessings I request for others:

T

D: _____ Blessings I request for myself:

W

D: _____ Scripture I can learn today:

T

D: _____ I am in awe of:

F

_____ Praying over the week and looking forward:

S

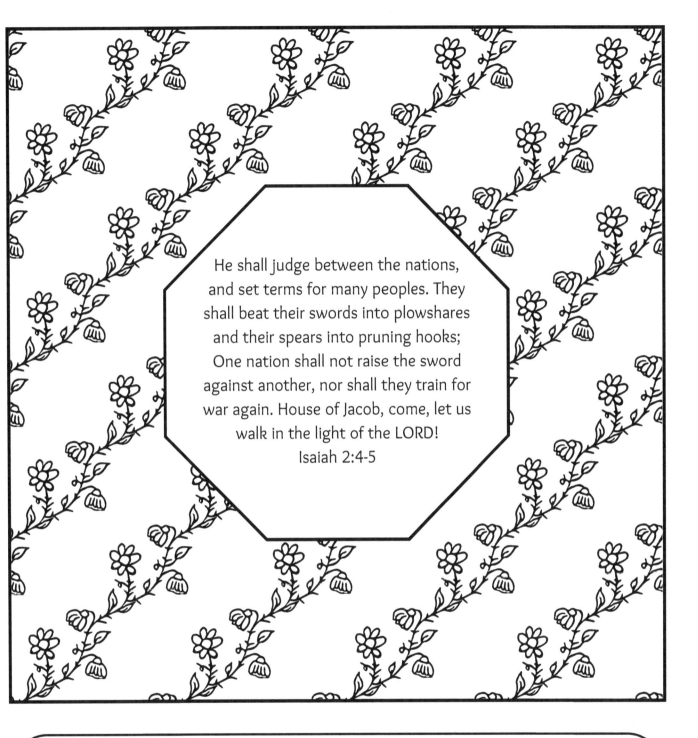

He shall judge between the nations, and set terms for many peoples. They shall beat their swords into plowshares and their spears into pruning hooks; One nation shall not raise the sword against another, nor shall they train for war again. House of Jacob, come, let us walk in the light of the LORD!

Isaiah 2:4-5

Reflection:

D: _____   Where can I ask for help?

S

D: _____   What is the greatest challenge God is setting for me right now?

M

D: _____   What is something I can give up for God?

T

D: _____   How can I do a better job of loving others?

W

D: _____   How can I do a better job of loving myself?

T

D: _____   Where can I provide help?

F

_____   Praying over the week and looking forward:

S

That abundance may flourish in his days, great bounty, till the moon be no more. For he rescues the poor when they cry out, the oppressed who have no one to help. He shows pity to the needy and the poor and saves the lives of the poor.

Psalms 72:7, 12-13

Reflection:

D: _____

S

Where am I feeling passion lead me lately?

D: _____

M

In my heart, do I feel that my passion aligns with God's purpose for me?

D: _____

T

How are my fears holding me back from following God's way?

D: _____

W

One step I can take to overcome my fear:

D: _____

T

One specific, actionable goal I can make to follow God's way:

D: _____

F

What am I deeply fearing?

_____

S

Praying over the week and looking forward:

Be patient, therefore, brothers, until the coming of the Lord. See how the farmer waits for the precious fruit of the earth, being patient with it until it receives the early and the late rains. You too must be patient. Make your hearts firm, because the coming of the Lord is at hand.

James 5:7-8

Reflection:

D: _____ Where has God led me over the last twelve weeks?

S

D: _____ How has my faith grown in the last twelve weeks?

M

D: _____ What patterns do I see in my reflections and prayers of last twelve weeks?

T

D: _____ Where do I sense God's presence pulling me for the next twelve weeks?

W

D: _____ How do I want to deepen my faith in the next twelve weeks?

T

D: _____ What are my goals and dreams for the next twelve weeks?

F

_____ Praying over the week and looking forward:

S

"Behold, the virgin shall be with child and bear
a son, and they shall name him Emmanuel."
Matthew 1:23

Reflection:

D: _____

S

Things I can learn today:

Reflections on the year

Our Father

Our Father,
Who art in heaven,
hallowed be Thy name.
Thy kingdom come,
Thy will be done, on earth as it is in heaven.
Give us this day our daily bread,
and forgive us our trespasses
as we forgive those who trespass against us,
and lead us not into temptation,
but deliver us from evil. Amen.

Hail Mary

Hail Mary, full of grace, the Lord is with thee.
Blessed art thou amongst women,
and blessed is the fruit of thy womb, Jesus.
Holy Mary, Mother of God,
pray for us sinners,
now and at the hour of our death. Amen.

Glory Be

Glory be to the Father,
and to the Son,
and to the Holy Spirit,
as it was in the beginning,
is now, and ever shall be,
world without end. Amen.

The Apostle's Creed

I believe in God,
the Father Almighty,
Creator of Heaven and earth;
and in Jesus Christ, His only Son, Our Lord,
Who was conceived by the Holy Spirit,
born of the Virgin Mary,
suffered under Pontius Pilate,
was crucified, died, and was buried.
He descended into Hell,
on the third day He arose again from the dead.
He ascended into Heaven,
and is seated at the right hand of
God the Father Almighty;
from thence He shall come to judge
the living and the dead.
I believe in the Holy Spirit,
the holy Catholic Church,
the communion of saints,
the forgiveness of sins,
the resurrection of the body,
and the life everlasting. Amen.

Hail Holy Queen

Hail, Holy Queen, Mother of mercy,
our life, our sweetness and our hope.
To thee do we cry,
poor banished children of Eve:
to thee do we send up our sighs,
mourning and weeping in this valley of tears.
Turn then, most gracious advocate,
thine eyes of mercy toward us,
and after this our exile,
show unto us the blessed
fruit of thy womb, Jesus.
O clement, O loving, O sweet Virgin Mary!
Pray for us, O holy Mother of God,
that we may be made worthy
of the promises of Christ. Amen.

Anima Christi

Soul of Christ, sanctify me,
Body of Christ, save me,
Blood of Christ, inebriate me,
Water from the side of Christ, wash me,
Passion of Christ, strengthen me,
O good Jesus, hear me.
Hide me within your wounds,
keep me close to you,
defend me from the evil enemy,
call me at the hour of my death,
and bid me to come to you,
to praise you with your saints,
forever and ever. Amen.

Memorare

Remember, O most gracious Virgin Mary,
that never was it known
that any one who fled to thy protection,
implored thy help,
or sought thy intercession,
was left unaided.
Inspired by this confidence,
We fly unto thee,
O Virgin of virgins my Mother;
to thee do we come, before thee we stand,
sinful and sorrowful,
O Mother of the Word Incarnate,
despise not our petitions,
but in thy mercy hear and answer them. Amen.

The Angelus

The Angel of the Lord declared unto Mary.
And she conceived by the Holy Spirit.
Hail Mary, full of grace...
Behold the handmaid of the Lord.
Be it done unto me according to thy word.
Hail Mary, full of grace...
And the Word was made Flesh.
And dwelt among us.
Hail Mary, full of grace...
Pray for us, O Holy Mother of God,
that we may be made worthy of the promises of Christ.
Let us pray. Pour forth, we beseech thee, O Lord, thy grace
into our hearts, that we, to whom the Incarnation of Christ,
thy son, was made known by the message of an angel, may by
his passion and cross be brought to the glory of his
resurrection, through the same Christ our Lord.
Amen.

Saint Michael Prayer

Saint Michael the Archangel,
defend us in battle.
Be our protection against
the wickedness and snares of the devil.
May God rebuke him, we humbly pray,
and do thou, O Prince of the heavenly host,
by the power of God,
cast into hell Satan and all the evil spirits
who prowl throughout the world
seeking the ruin of souls.
Amen.

Act of Contrition

O my God, I am heartfully sorry for having offended thee, and I
detest all my sins because of thy just punishment, but most of
all because I have offended thee my God, who is all good and
deserving of all my love. I firmly resolve, with the help of thy
grace, to sin no more, and to avoid the near occasion of sin.
Amen.

Miraculous Medal Prayer

O Mary, Conceived without Sin, pray for us who have recourse
to thee, and for those who do not have recourse to thee,
especially the enemies of the Church.
Amen.

Morning Offering

Dear Lord, I do not know what will happen to me today —
I only know that nothing will happen that was not foreseen
by you and directed to my greater good from all eternity. I
adore your holy and unfathomable plans, and submit to
them with all my heart for love of you, the pope, and the
Immaculate Heart of Mary. Amen.

Guardian Angel Prayer

Angel of God, my guardian dear, to whom God's love
commits me here, ever this day be at my side, to light and
guard, to rule and guide. Amen.

Prayer of Surrender

Lord Jesus Christ, take all my freedom, my understanding,
and my will. All that I have and cherish you have given to
me. I surrender it all to be guided by your will. Your love
and your grace are wealth enough for me. Give me these,
Lord Jesus, and I ask for nothing more.
Amen.

Grace Before Meals

Bless us, O Lord, and these thy gifts, which we are about
to receive, from thy bounty, through Christ our Lord.
Amen.

Grace After Meals

We give thee thanks for all thy benefits, O Almighty God,
who lives and reigns, world without end. Amen.
May the souls of the faithful departed, through the mercy
of God, rest in peace.
Amen.

Sign of the Cross

In the name of the Father,
and of the Son,
and of the Holy Spirit.
Amen.

Made in United States
Troutdale, OR
12/07/2023

15507612R00064